THE LITTLE BOOK OF
SAN FRANCISCO

Published in 2022 by OH!
An Imprint of Welbeck Non-Fiction Limited,
part of Welbeck Publishing Group.
Based in London and Sydney.
www.welbeckpublishing.com

Compilation text © Welbeck Non-Fiction Limited 2022
Design © Welbeck Non-Fiction Limited 2022

ISBN 978-1-80069-188-9

Compiled and written by: Japhet Asher
Editorial: Victoria Denne
Project manager: Russell Porter
Design: Tony Seddon
Production: Jess Brisley

A CIP catalogue record for this book is available from the British Library

Printed in China

10 9 8 7 6 5 4 3 2 1

Images: Shutterstock

THE LITTLE BOOK OF
SAN FRANCISCO

A CITY THAT WILL CAPTURE
YOUR HEART

CONTENTS

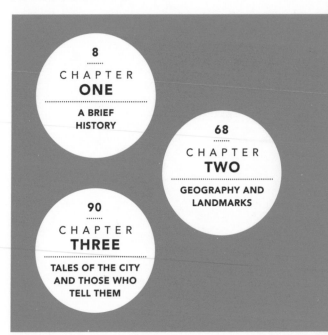

INTRODUCTION

"The city isn't like it used to be," long-time residents say about San Francisco, neck and neck with New York for America's highest cost of living, as new arrivals share stories about the stratospheric price of a place to sleep or a loaf of sourdough bread. Yet San Francisco is also exactly what it has always been—an open-minded and open-hearted city that changes with every generation of newcomers.

San Francisco is perhaps America's greatest hotbed of invention. The birthplace of the blue jean, television and the Twitter hashtag, the Beat Generation and the Hippies, the United Nations and the Pride Parade, San Francisco has been shaped by waves of discovery and change, both in its geography and its residents. The history of the city includes the Gold Rush, the massive earthquakes of '06 and '89, the Summer of Love, the battle for gay rights and a cure for AIDS, the disruption of dot-coms and tech giants.

Yet the essential San Francisco remains the same place the Spanish missionaries found back in 1776, a jewel of a city constrained and protected by its peninsula of land jutting out into the Bay where Otis Redding sat on his dock. It turns out, San Francisco's greatest invention is itself.

San Francisco sits on a peninsula of stunning vistas, vibrant neighborhoods, steep climbs and crooked streets, tech behemoths and corner cafés, Chinatown and Russian Hill, mysterious characters and romantic cable cars, all blanketed most evenings by a layer of fog locals call Karl. The City's revered columnist Herb Caen spoke for all residents of San Francisco when he said: "One day if I go to heaven … I'll look around and say, 'It ain't bad, but it ain't San Francisco.'"

This book is for all those who have yet to fall in love with the City by the Bay, and for all those who have already left their heart there.

CHAPTER

1

A Brief History

The history of San Francisco is a story of seismic change, on the ground and in its people.

Mission Dolores

As the American colonies declared independence from Britain in 1776, Spanish missionaries founded the Mission Dolores around which San Francisco was built.

The mission has persevered
through the Gold Rush,
devastating earthquakes,
two World Wars, the cultural
upheavals of the '60s and '70s,
the financial shocks of the
dot-com bust and the
Tech Boom.

And so has San Francisco.

❝

San Francisco values did
not come into the world with
flowers in their hair; they
were born howling, in
blood and strife … One of
San Francisco's more flowery
laureates anointed it 'the
cool gray city of love.' But
the people who cling to

its hills and hollows and know its mercurial temperament—the sudden juggernaut of sea fog and wind that can shroud the sun and chill the soul—recognize San Francisco as a rougher beast.

99

David Talbot, journalist, in his book
Season of the Witch

The earliest archaeological evidence of humans living in the territory of the city of San Francisco dates back to 4000 BC.

Foreshadowing the "foodie" reputation of their descendants, early San Franciscans over-indulged in mussels and oysters, leaving millions of shells in mounds to be discovered in the early 20th century.

Yelamu villagers of the Ohlone people lived locally when a Spanish exploration party led by Don Gaspar de Portolá arrived on November 2, 1769, becoming the first European tourists to visit San Francisco.

"

As many of you know, I come from San Francisco. We don't have a lot of farms there. Well, we do have one—it's a mushroom farm, so you know what that means.

"

House Speaker Nancy Pelosi, speaking to the Washington Agribusiness Club

The San Francisco Bay could
have been first "discovered" by
the Elizabethan explorer Francis
Drake. His ship the *Golden Hind*
stopped for repairs at Point Reyes,
just north of the present-day
city, on June 17, 1579.

It's said that Francis and his men
planted a wooden sign with a

brass plaque on California soil,
naming the land New Albion and
claiming it for Elizabeth I.

But Francis sailed right past
San Francisco Bay itself and went
on down the coast and onwards
around the globe, never knowing
what he missed. A few years later,
he was knighted by the Queen and
beat back the Spanish Armada's
attack on Britain.

But New Albion was forgotten.

San Francisco

The magnificent city is named for Saint Francis of Assisi, while Sir Francis Drake has a small beach named after him on the other side of the Bay, where there are a few picnic tables and a visitors' centre.

As the original east coast American states declared independence from Britain in 1776, Spanish colonists founded a settlement, establishing a military base at the Presidio of San Francisco at the Golden Gate and a religious centre at Mission San Francisco de Asís, a few miles away.

Mission San Francisco de Asís is commonly known as Mission Dolores after the name of a creek that once ran nearby.

The Mission's garden still grows native plant species from the 18th century, while inside, a mural painted in 1791 by Ohlone artisans was recently found, hidden but preserved by the altar.

Spanish San Francisco became part of Mexico in the 1821 War of Mexican Independence, before joining the USA in 1848, just as the Gold Rush changed the city forever.

Yerba Buena

San Francisco was originally called Yerba Buena under Mexican rule.

Yerba Buena, an aromatic plant belonging to the mint family, translates into English as 'Good Herb'.

It's said this can still be found in San Francisco.

In 1835, William Richardson, a naturalized Mexican citizen of English birth, erected the first independent homestead in Yerba Buena near a boat anchorage around what is now Chinatown.

Together with Alcalde Francisco de Haro, he laid out a street plan for the expanded settlement of a few hardy pioneers.

Gold Rush

On January 24, 1848, mill owner John Sutter and his carpenter James Marshall found flakes of gold in a streambed along the American River north of San Francisco.

They agreed to become
partners and keep their find
a secret. It didn't work.

Within weeks, thousands
of fortune-seekers
had descended on Sutter's
land and the Gold Rush
had begun.

As news spread,
the population of
San Francisco rose from
1,000 in 1848 to 25,000
in 1849.

Gold Rush prospectors became known as Forty Niners. A hundred years later, San Francisco's new pro football team took the same name. Their cheerleaders?

The Gold Rush.

The promise of great wealth was so strong that crews on arriving vessels deserted and rushed off to the gold fields, leaving behind a forest of masts in San Francisco harbor.

Some of these approximately 500 abandoned ships were used at times as storeships, saloons, and hotels.

With his property overrun
and his goods and livestock
stolen or destroyed, John Sutter
was bankrupt by 1852. But at
least Sutter has an important
San Francisco street named
after him, whereas James
Marshall, who also ended up
destitute, does not.

Among the Goldrush miners was a young Mark Twain. Like 99% of prospectors, he made no money at all from gold. The ones who struck it rich were those who catered to their dreams.

Wrote Twain: "A mine is a hole in the ground with a liar standing next to it."

66

When everybody is digging for gold, it's good to be in the pick and shovel business.

99

Attributed to Mark Twain

Chinatown

The Gold Rush also brought the first wave of Chinese immigrants to the city.

San Francisco's Chinatown is the oldest and largest in North America.

At the time, it was the only area of the City where Chinese people were allowed to live. And it was primarily settled by men, as immigration laws made it hard for Chinese women to come with them.

People say Levi Strauss made his fortune selling jeans to miners. But he was actually selling canvas trousers.

He didn't make his first pair of riveted blue jeans from denim until twenty years later.

Banks flourished in the
Gold Rush. Wells Fargo, now the
third largest bank in America,
was formed as a delivery service
for letters and parcels, but rapidly
became a trusted way to handle
payments between distant parties, a
precursor to PayPal, invented
150 years later just down the
Peninsula in San Jose.

The Big Four

The Transcontinental Railroad reached San Francisco in 1869. It changed life for all San Franciscans but it benefitted four men most of all, known as the Big Four: Leland Stanford, Collis Huntington, Mark Hopkins and Charles Crocker.

The Big Four owned the
Southern Pacific Railroad,
which held a monopoly on goods
coming through the city to and
from the port.

Their business stranglehold was
known locally as the Octopus,
and its owners as Nabobs, later
shortened to Nobs.

The four built opulent mansions the size of castles in the neighborhood now called Nob Hill.

Crocker built not one but two mansions—one for his son as a wedding present. He ran into a problem, however, when a stubborn German undertaker named Nicholas Yung would not sell his property to accommodate the Crocker spread.

Crocker, enraged, retaliated by building a 40-foot fence around the back of Yung's house, obliterating sunlight and Yung's view of the city.

The notorious "Spite Fence" became a rallying point for San Francisco citizenry as a symbol of big business oppression of the common man, setting the stage for contemporary city politics.

Earthquake!

By April 17, 1906,
San Francisco was a city
of over 400,000, the
centre of finance, culture
and commerce for
America's West.

At 5.12 a.m. on April 18, 1906, a major earthquake struck San Francisco and northern California.

As buildings collapsed from the shaking, ruptured gas lines ignited fires that spread across the city and burned out of control for several days.

More than three quarters of the city was destroyed—90% by the fires after the shaking stopped.

It's estimated 3,000 died and 200,000 were left homeless.

In an effort to slow
the fires, the army even
destroyed

30,000

bottles of liquor.

(Or so they claimed.)

When the stock market
crash of 1929, and the
Great Depression that followed,
ravaged the rest of America,
San Francisco was in the
midst of its reconstruction,
building the Golden Gate and
Bay Bridges and reinventing
itself once again.

"

There you are –
electronic television!

"

Philo Farnsworth, to his assistants in his
workshop at 202 Green Street upon successfully
demonstrating his invention for the first time in
September, 1927

Alcatraz

Alcatraz Island was originally called "La Isla de los Alcatraces", or the "Island of the Pelicans".

In the 1930s, the federal government began using Alcatraz for the housing of high-level prisoners, notably killers like Al Capone and Robert Stroud, the "Birdman of Alcatraz".

Perhaps the cruelest
punishment for the hardcore
criminals held on Alcatraz was
that some nights they could
smell the cooking and hear the
music and laughter from
the clubs and restaurants of
Fisherman's Wharf, carried
out to their cells on a ghost
of a breeze.

Government records show that 1,647,174 passengers—soldiers, sailors, Marines and civilians like Red Cross personnel—boarded ships at Fort Mason bound for the Pacific.

Two thirds of all the troops sent to the Pacific in World War II passed through San Francisco. Many returned to live near the city at war's end.

66

If we do not want to die together in war, we must learn to live together in peace.

99

President Harry Truman, as he convened the conference in San Francisco that would result in the United Nations Charter creating the UN in 1945

In the years that followed its central role in World War II and the founding of the UN, San Francisco became a magnet for America's counterculture.

In the 1950s, Beat Generation writers congregated in San Francisco in search of literary gold, or at least a decent espresso.

"

It seemed like a matter of minutes when we began rolling in the foothills before Oakland and suddenly reached a height and saw stretched out ahead of us the fabulous white city of San Francisco on her eleven mystic hills with the blue Pacific and its advancing wall of potato-patch fog beyond, and smoke and goldenness in the late afternoon of time.

"

Jack Kerouac, *On the Road*

The Summer of Love

The Summer of Love didn't begin in the summer, but on January 14, 1967, at the Human Be-In in Golden Gate Park.

It featured speeches rejecting middle-class values by Timothy Leary and Ram Dass,

poetry from Allen Ginsberg, free LSD made by Owsley Stanley, turkeys provided by the Diggers, and music by the Grateful Dead, Jefferson Airplane and Janis Joplin.

The Human Be-In's message was broadcast to the world. Millions heard the call.

"

Turn On, Tune In, Drop Out.

"

Timothy Leary, speaking at the Human Be-In
that kicked off the age of psychedelics and the
Summer of Love

It's estimated that over 100,000 "flower children" descended on the Haight-Ashbury neighborhood in just the summer of 1967, turning the area into a vast social experiment.

In 1974, the Zebra
murders left at least
16 people dead.

The Age of Aquarius
in San Francisco
was over.

Gay Rights

In the 1970s, the city became a centre of the gay rights movement, with the emergence of the Castro as an urban gay village and the election of Harvey Milk to the Board of Supervisors, making him the first openly gay elected official in the United States.

"

If a bullet should enter my brain, let that bullet destroy every closet door.

"

Harvey Milk

Harvey Milk was assassinated with Mayor George Moscone in 1978 by fellow supervisor Dan White, an opponent of gay rights, who claimed that eating too many Twinkies made him do it.

What Dan White could not do, the AIDS virus did instead, decimating San Francisco's LQBTQ community in the 1980s.

But out of the suffering came both a more humane and supportive treatment of HIV/AIDS worldwide known as the "San Francisco Model" as well as a fiercer activism for change.

"

Such was life in the
Golden Gate:

Gold dusted all we
drank and ate,

And I was one of the
children told,

'We all must eat our
peck of gold.'

"

Robert Frost, native San Franciscan, capturing the
essence of the golden state of the city from his poem
Peck of Gold, published in 1928

The Digital Revolution

The internet that changed
San Francisco all over again was
significantly shaped by early
adopters of the technology from
San Francisco's counterculture,
notably Stewart Brand, creator
of the *Whole Earth Catalog*,
and his visionary online

community The WELL … but they lost control of their ideals.

As one of the WELL's members, *Wired Magazine* co-founder Louis Rossetto, wrote in the first issue of his new magazine:

"the Digital Revolution is whipping through our lives like a Bengali typhoon."

During the dot-com boom of the 1990s, it's estimated that 70% of San Francisco's long-time residents left the city in the face of spiralling costs of living and a new, cutthroat start-up culture that the original 49ers might have recognized but the Baby Boom Be-In generation did not.

When the dot-com bubble burst, internet stocks lost

1.75 trillion dollars

of value and 48% of businesses in the sector went bust. But the seeds of San Francisco's subsequent tech boom were planted in the soil of dot-com decay.

CHAPTER

2

Geography and Landmarks

People come to San Francisco for opportunities, but they stay for the awesome natural beauty, magical light, unique landmarks and open-hearted lifestyle that make San Francisco irresistible.

San Francisco is at the edge of the continent, but it's also its own little world, separate somehow in geography and in spirit from the rest of America.

Of course, if movement in the earth's crust has its way, San Francisco may yet break away all together.

"

San Francisco
is 49 square miles
surrounded by
reality.

"

Jefferson Airplane's Paul Kantner

San Francisco lies between two potential earthquake fault lines.

The lesser known is the Hayward fault, but the San Andreas fault caused both the 1906 and 1989 earthquakes.

There are around

5,000

earthquakes every year in
the San Francisco area,
but most are so small you
won't notice them.

The city is built on
50 hills, and also
encompasses 5 islands.

The city limits stretch
27 miles out into the
Pacific Ocean to include
the Farallon Islands, an
uninhabited nature reserve.

The total square mileage
of the city and county of
San Francisco is 257. However,
183 of those are under water.

What most people consider
the city is a roughly
7 x 7- mile square on a
peninsula of land jutting out
into the Bay.

The Golden Gate Bridge is constantly being painted in its iconic red colour. By the time painters cover one end of the bridge, it's time to start again at the other. The Golden Gate was originally planned by the US military to be painted in yellow and black stripes.

The Marina District was
once part of the Bay and is
built entirely on landfill.
It is one of three San Francisco
neighborhoods created in
this way.

During the 1989 quake, the
landfill "liquified" with
shockwaves, resulting in much
greater damage in those areas.

Lombard Street on Russian Hill, known as the World's Crookedest Street®, is beautiful, but it isn't even San Francisco's crookedest street.

That would be Vermont Street on Potrero Hill between 20th and 22nd Streets. It's not as picturesque as Lombard, but definitely has steeper curves.

The Bay Bridge between San Francisco and Oakland was completed a year after the Golden Gate, in 1937. It partially collapsed in the 1989 Loma Prieta quake.

Tourists aren't the only visitors to Fisherman's Wharf.
A pack of sea lions took up residence at Pier 39 after the Loma Prieta quake and have been serenading the locals with their barks ever since.

Alamo Square is famous for its row of seven identically built Victorian homes known as either the Painted Ladies or the Seven Sisters. The houses feature in the title sequence to the TV sitcom *Full House*, hundreds of tourism brochures and millions of Instagram selfies.

The Salesforce Tower

Completed in 2018 the Salesforce Tower, formerly know as the Transbay Tower, displaced the iconic Transamerica Pyramid as the San Francisco's tallest building with an overall height of 1,070 feet (335 m)

Its top nine floors have been sheathed in 11,000 lights and video screens that allow an art installation showing daily scenes of city life to be displayed all night long.

The screens are visible from almost anywhere in San Francisco and were converted into the Eye of Sauron (of *Lord of the Rings* fame) one year for Halloween.

The shape of Coit Tower atop Telegraph Hill reminds some people of a fireman's hose nozzle. It's claimed that this is coincidental, but it is certainly the case that Lady Hitchcock Coit was a huge admirer of the Fire Department and built the tower in their honour.

The Palace of Fine Arts,
north of the Marina, was built
out of temporary materials
for the 1915 Panama Pacific
Explosion, but proved so
popular that it was maintained,
and then completely rebuilt to
the exact same specifications
in the 1960s.

The Dragon's Gate at the entrance to Chinatown is engraved with a saying from Sun Yat-sen:

"All under Heaven is for the good of the people".

The California Palace of the Legion of Honor is an exact replica of the Palais de la Legion d'Honneur in Paris. The benefactor who funded its construction was clearly a big fan of the French.

The building houses a museum of primarily European art and an enormous symphonic organ.

Union Square is at the heart of the city's downtown shop and hotel district.

Maiden Lane, now a side street of high-priced clothing boutiques off the Square, was once reputed to be the address of commercial establishments where clothing was optional.

The San Francisco Giants baseball team moved into a new home in China Basin called Oracle Park in 2000.

The stadium sits right on the Bay. Fans in kayaks and dinghies float in McCovey Cove, named after a former Giant great, to capture balls hit out of the stadium into the Bay for home runs.

The team had hit close to a hundred homers into McCovey Cove as of 2021.

CHAPTER

3

Tales of the City and Those Who Tell Them

San Francisco has some of the world's finest art museums, but much of its best culture can be found in its streets and communities or shown on screens the world over.

City Lights Bookstore, heart of the Beat Generation, is the first culture stop for many visitors, but just a block away is the home of Francis Ford Coppola's American Zoetrope film studio.

Street performances, wall murals and movie locations are easy to find, because the city is both home to famous and emerging artists and a favorite location for their art.

In 1953, poet Lawrence Ferlinghetti founded City Lights Bookstore in North Beach.

It became the cultural nexus of the Beat Generation and went on to global fame after Ferlinghetti's arrest in 1956 for publishing Allen Ginsberg's sexually frank poem epic, *Howl*.

US customs officers seized an early printing of the book, and Ferlinghetti was arrested on charges of publishing obscene material when two undercover cops bought a copy at City Lights.

Howl remains a top seller at the store.

❝

I saw the best minds of my generation
destroyed by madness, starving
hysterical naked,

dragging themselves through the negro
streets at dawn looking for an angry fix,

angel headed hipsters burning for the
ancient heavenly connection to the starry
dynamo in the machinery of night,

who poverty and tatters and hollow-
eyed and high sat up smoking in the
supernatural darkness of cold-water
flats floating across the tops of cities
contemplating jazz,

who bared their brains to Heaven
under the El and saw Mohammedan
angels staggering on tenement roofs
illuminated,

who passed through universities with
radiant cool eyes hallucinating Arkansas
and Blake-light tragedy among the
scholars of war ...

"

**Allen Ginsberg's lament for 'the Lamb in America' from
his poem *Howl*, published in 1956**

66

San Francisco itself is
art, above all literary art.
Every block is a short
story, every hill a novel.
Every home a poem, every
dweller within immortal.

99

William Saroyan, novelist

The angular Sentinel Building, just down Columbus Avenue from City Lights, is home to Francis Ford Coppola's American Zoetrope.

From this building, he made films including *The Godfather Part 2*, *Apocalypse Now* and *The Conversation*. Plus the café downstairs features his winemaking exploits as well.

The baroque Victorian house at 507 Divisadero is the real-world address of the location where the fictional Lestat was interviewed in Anne Rice's novel, *Interview with the Vampire*.

❝

'I see–' said the vampire thoughtfully, and slowly he walked across the room towards the window. For a long time he stood there against the dim light from Divisadero Street and the passing beams of traffic.

The boy could see the furnishings of the room more clearly now, the round oak table, the chairs. A wash basin hung on one wall with a mirror. He set his briefcase on the table and waited.

'But how much tape do you have with you?' asked the vampire, turning now so the boy could see his profile. 'Enough for the story of a life?'

Anne Rice, *Interview with the Vampire*

There's a plaque mounted on Burritt Street, a side alley on the back side of Nob Hill, that reads, "On approximately this spot, Miles Archer, partner of Sam Spade, was done in by Brigid O'Shaughnessy."

Of course, Miles Archer, Sam Spade and Brigid O'Shaughnessy are not historical characters, but the creations of author Dashiell Hammett, and the death of Miles Archer is a moment in the film *The Maltese Falcon.* This alleyway is only a few blocks away from Hammett's actual apartment, one which he shared with his fictional gumshoe Spade, who also lived at 891 Post Street.

You can still order Sam Spade's meal at John's Grill on Ellis Street, the spot where he planned his next move after Miles Archer was gunned down:

"

He went to John's Grill, asked the waiter to hurry his order of chops, baked potato, and sliced tomatoes, ate hurriedly, and was smoking a cigarette with his coffee when a thick-set youngish man with a plaid cap set askew above pale eyes and a tough cheery face came into the Grill and to his table.

'All set, Mr. Spade. She's full of gas and rearing to go.'

Armistead Maupin began writing *Tales of the City*, his series of novels set in San Francisco, as a newspaper column about the residents of a fictional address on Russian Hill, 28 Barbary Lane.

San Franciscans recognised the oasis run by magical, marijuana-growing landlady Anna Madrigal as a doppelgänger for houses on Macondray Lane, which was used as the location for the TV version.

"

Some people drink
to forget.
Personally, I smoke
to remember.

"

Anna Madrigal, *Tales of the City*

The best street art in all of San Francisco can be seen at Balmy Alley.

It's located in the Mission District and is filled with murals. Almost every building here is completely covered.

"

Los Angeles? That's
just a big parking
lot where you buy a
hamburger for a trip
to San Francisco.

"

John Lennon

Since the beginning of talking pictures in 1929, San Francisco has been Hollywood's favorite movie location with over 300 movies filmed in the city. Here's one from every decade:

After the Thin Man (1936)

The Maltese Falcon (1941)

Vertigo (1958)

Guess Who's Coming to Dinner (1967)

The Conversation (1974)

Star Trek IV – The Voyage Home (1986)

Mrs Doubtfire (1993)

The Pursuit of Happyness (2006)

The Last Black Man in San Francisco (2019)

The *San Francisco Chronicle's* list of top SF movie car chases

The Rock (1996)

The Lineup (1958)

What's Up, Doc? (1972)

Ant Man and the Wasp (2018)

The Dead Pool (1988)

Bullitt (1968)

The "Grateful Dead House" in the Haight-Ashbury is where the band lived during the Summer of Love and remains a mecca for visiting Deadheads. The house at 710 Ashbury Street is currently a private home, as is the one-time Hells Angels house across the street at 715, where Jerry Garcia reportedly hid when the police raided his home and arrested his band mates for drug possession.

Some memorable lines from San Francisco movie characters

Father Mullin: "You're in probably the wickedest, most corrupt city, most Godless city in America. Sometimes it frightens me. I wonder what the end's going to be."

San Francisco (1936)
starring Clark Gable, Jeanette MacDonald and Spencer Tracy

Scottie: What's this doohickey?
Midge: It's a brassiere! You know about those things, you're a big boy now.

Vertigo (1958)
starring Jimmie Stewart and Kim Novak

Daniel: "God bless you. You know I'm feeling fabulous because I met this beautiful Cuban. Every night is like the Bay of Pigs."

Mrs Doubtfire (1994)
starring Robin Williams

Harry Callahan: "Go ahead. Make my day."

Harry Callahan: "Magnum, the most powerful handgun in the world, and would blow your head clean off, you've got to ask yourself one question: Do I feel lucky? Well, do ya, punk?"

Dirty Harry (1972)
starring Clint Eastwood

10 bands to come out of the SF music scene

The Grateful Dead

Jefferson Airplane

Santana

Sly and the Family Stone

Creedence Clearwater Revival

Journey

Metallica

Green Day

Huey Lewis and the News

Faith No More

Longtime San Franciscan Bobby McFerrin wrote his hit song *"Don't Worry, Be Happy"* in the city, but the title originates from a saying by Indian mystic Meher Baba, which appeared on posters in San Francisco in the 1960s.

Top 10 songs about San Francisco

(according to destinationsoundtrack.com)

I Left My Heart in San Francisco
Tony Bennett

The epitome of San Francisco anthems, Bennett's love letter to the City by the Bay is also his own signature song. It's one of San Francisco's two official songs.

Fake Tales of San Francisco
Arctic Monkeys

Released in 2005, this song was one of the earliest from the British indie rock band and derides a fictional band for its falsely cited San Francisco and U.S. imagery.

San Francisco
(Be Sure To Wear Flowers in Your Hair)
Scott McKenzie

Released in 1967 to promote the Monterey Pop
Festival, this hit song inspired thousands of
young people to head to the city in the late '60s.

Save Me, San Francisco
Train

Catchy and rocking, Train's title song from
their 2009 album reads like a neighborhood
tour of the City by the Bay.

San Francisco
Judy Garland

Garland covers the title song from a 1936 film
about the 1906 San Francisco earthquake—one
of the two official songs of San Francisco.

San Francisco Bay Blues
Eric Clapton

Clapton covered Jesse Fuller's classic blues track on *MTV's Unplugged* in 1992. The show and its subsequent Grammy-winning album made the song his to a generation.

Come Back From San Francisco
Magnetic Fields

The Magnetic Fields pine for a distant love to return to New York City from the temptations of San Francisco in this pleasant alternative track.

(Sittin' on the) Dock of the Bay
Otis Redding

Yep, it's that bay. Well, sort of. Redding was on a houseboat in Sausalito when he wrote this song. He recorded it a few days before he died.

Grace Catherdral Hill
The Decemberists

Lead singer Colin Meloy reminisces about a moment experienced at and around the landmark Grace Cathedral on Nob Hill.

San Francisco Days
Chris Issak

Isaak can't let go of a love from San Francisco in this 1993 soft-rock track.

CHAPTER

4

Worlds to Discover Indoors and Out

Apparently Mark Twain never said, "The coldest winter I ever spent was a summer in San Francisco," but he would only have been exaggerating slightly had he done so.

Hot air inland pulls cool air and moisture in from the Pacific, keeping San Francisco temperatures much lower than surrounding cities.

Plus there are microclimates across the City's hills and valleys, so locals know to dress in layers and always have indoor and outdoor plans in every season.

The California Academy of Sciences incorporates four separate museums, covering the bottom of the oceans to the far reaches of the stars.

Steinhart Aquarium

Kimball Natural History Museum

Osher Rainforest

Morrison Planetarium

Golden Gate Park

Over 3 miles long, San Francisco's large urban park is bigger than New York's Central Park. The Park incorporates the de Young Museum, the California Academy of Sciences, a Japanese Tea Garden, and the boathouse at Stowe Lake.

A scavenger hunt could uncover a Victorian carousel, windmills, an aquarium, an arboretum, and, most unusual of all, a herd of bison.

The first buffalo was brought to the park in 1890, a rare survivor of what were once immense herds across the West.

"

To get an idea of the way
bison behave, you should
know that the position of
their tail greatly alerts others
to what the creature is doing
or thinking he or she will
do next … When the tail is
slightly raised, the bison is
displaying mild excitement.

As the animal fills with nervousness, the tail will arch, often followed by a bowel movement. When the tail is raised in a vertical position, a bison challenge may arise.

99

Excerpt from the official Golden Gate Park website

The de Young Museum

Located in Golden Gate Park, de Young Museum is the 6th most visited museum in the USA. Founded in 1895, it was once known as both the leading museum of Asian Art in America, as well as having a prodigious collection of American artworks.

After a huge renovation in 2005, its Asian Art Museum was moved to another location, and the de Young refocused on its equally significant collection of American artists and Arts of the Americas, and is now the most visited art museum in San Francisco.

The new Asian Art Museum near the Civic Center is where those Asian art collections now reside.

Established in what was originally San Francisco's main public library, the building houses over 18,000 pieces, including some over 6,000 years old.

The Pagoda at the Japanese Tea Garden in Golden Gate Park was originally built as a temporary display for the same Expo in 1915 as the Palace of Fine Arts, and was also converted into a permanent San Francisco feature and moved to the Tea Garden.

You can actually drink tea in the garden of course, but it's known primarily as a tranquil spot for meditation.

The Exploratorium

Situated on San Francisco's Embarcadero near Pier 39, the Exploratorium is the most popular museum in San Francisco, and certainly the most unique.

It more than lives up to its Mission statement:

"

The Exploratorium is a public
learning laboratory exploring
the world through science, art,
and human perception.

"

In practice, that means exhibits
you can play with, designed
by artists to explain scientific
principles. Amazing.

The Presidio

This fortified location was a military base for over 218 years for the Spanish, Mexican and finally US armies. But since 1994, the base has been a national park. While its history is still traceable along its trails, it's now an urban forest with many scenic vistas overlooking the Golden Gate Bridge, the Bay and the Pacific Ocean.

Ocean Beach

Part of the Golden Gate National Recreation Ares, Ocean Beach is the westernmost point of the city on the mainland.

It's the city's longest beach too, and is popular with serious surfers and dangerous for wet-suited swimmers, both because of its riptides.

Baker Beach was originally called the Golden Gate Milk Farm when it was owned by the Baker family.

You won't see any dairy cows there, but you do get great views of the Golden Gate. Baker Beach was also the original site for the Burning Man festival, back in the late 1980s.

66

When I was in my late 30s,
I lit a figure on fire on Baker
Beach in San Francisco.
It was me, a friend, and maybe
eight people, tops. There
wasn't any premeditation to
it at all. It was really just a
product of the San Franciscan
bohemian milieu.

99

Larry Harvey, Burning Man founder

Angel Island

The largest island in the Bay, Angel Island, has a chequered history. It was an immigration site from 1910 until 1940, primarily for ethnic Chinese. During World War II, Angel Island was used to confine military prisoners.

From 1955 until 1962, Angel Island was also used as a radar missile site. But today, the most prominent technology is a fitness tracker, as visitors hike, cycle and, in the parlance of our times, chill.

CHAPTER

5

Getting Around San Francisco

You don't have to take a cable car to move around SF (though if you want to, it's worth knowing that they stop for passengers at every intersection on their route, where you can get on board without waiting in the long queues at the terminal).

Public Transport

The headquarters of both Uber and Lyft are in San Francisco, but the Muni bus and trolley system is cheap and efficient, as is BART, the train line that connects SF to the East Bay.

But if you are willing
to walk the city's many
hills, you'll be rewarded
by making your own
discoveries from among
the independent shops and
sidewalk cafés that line
the city streets.

Facts about San Francisco's cable cars

The cars run at 9.5 miles per hour.

They wear through their track brakes every three days.

These track brakes are wooden, made of Douglas Fir.

This accounts for the smell of burning pine that riders sometimes notice along the tracks.

Cable Car gripmen need both strength
and delicacy. Strength to control the
brake lever on the steepest inclines,
and delicacy to ring out their signature
rhythm on the cable car's bell.
An annual prize is awarded for the
best bell ringer.

Excellence at braking is its
own reward.

Beyond cable cars, there are also still vintage "street cars" run by Muni, SF's transit system.

The F line runs all the way from Pier 39 to the Castro, and the E from the Embarcadero to Oracle Park.

Muni buses run a transfer system allowing the rider to switch between lines on a continuous journey.

Tech company shuttles share the bus lanes but don't share rides.

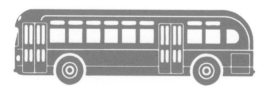

From the Ferry Building, you can catch ferries across the bay to Sausalito and Tiburon for waterside restaurants and bars, or to Angel Island for hiking and bike trails. But the ferries to Alcatraz leave from Fisherman's Wharf – make sure to buy a round-trip ticket!

There are signs along some SF streets featuring a seagull against a blue sky to mark out the 49 Mile Drive, a route to take in scenic vistas across the City.

Unfortunately, the signs—designed through a contest in 1954—are so regularly stolen that sections of the drive are hard to follow.

Chinatown

San Francisco has more than one Chinatown. The original, centred around Grant Avenue near downtown, is the oldest Chinatown in America, but starting in the 1950s, new immigrants from Asia began to settle along Clement Street in the Richmond district.

San Francisco's Japantown was at one time among the largest communities of Japanese outside Japan, but the population returned in much smaller numbers after the forced internment of ethnic Japanese during World War II.

The Chinese fortune cookie was invented by a Japanese resident of San Francisco.

North Beach

Not a beach but a neighborhood,
North Beach retains some of its
original Italian flavour, notably in
cafés like the Caffe Trieste, where
the Beatniks once drank their
espresso, and Mario's Bohemian
Cigar Store, where you can eat
sandwiches made with fresh
focaccia bread from the Liguria
Bakery nearby.

Washington Square, in the heart of North Beach, is the ultimate urban oasis, where seniors practice Tai Chi in the shade of St Peter's and Paul's Church, buskers play to pigeons, and the aroma of focaccia wafts from the Liguria ovens.

The Castro was the world's first urban gay village, and it remains the centre of the LGBTQ+ community in the city. Its best landmark is the marquee of the Castro Movie Theatre, a truly old-time picture palace in the silver screen tradition.

Take the Stairs

Thanks to its many hills, SF also has several famous staircases for pedestrians.

The mosaic stairs, ones where ceramics on the steps reveal mural art when seen from the bottom, include the Hidden Garden Steps at 16th Avenue and the Lincoln Park Steps.

The Filbert Street steps, a series of narrow wooden stairs through gorgeous gardens, and the Greenwhich steps lead you up and down Telegraph Hill.

And there's a Sand Ladder path between Crissy Field and the Golden Gate Bridge.

Neighborhoods

The San Francisco Planning Commission officially identifies 36 neighborhoods in San Francisco, which can be further broken down into some 119 micro-districts.

It truly is a city of neighborhood communities—each with its own character and personalities.

San Francisco's intensely competitive and tight housing market means that the character, boundaries and even names of city neighborhoods can change rapidly. But in some areas of SF, characteristics seem baked into neighborhood sidewalks and are gently absorbed by those who choose to live there.

Favorite San Francisco Neighborhoods

Russian Hill/Nob Hill
for the steepest hills and best views

Pacific Heights/Cow Hollow
for a taste of wealth and privilege

SOMA
for art galleries, dance clubs and tech company HQs

North Beach/Chinatown
for street life and café culture

Haight-Ashbury/Hayes Valley
for the counterculture

The Castro and Upper Market
for parades, street fairs and festivals

The Mission
for the best weather … those first
San Franciscans back in 1776 knew
what was what!

CHAPTER
6

Secret
San Francisco

Strange laws, hidden
places, weird happenings,
and odd characters
help earn San Francisco
its bohemian reputation.

San Francisco's fog may have a name (Karl) and its own Twitter feed, but it can still hide the city's secrets in its blanket.

"

I can walk down the streets of San Francisco, and here I'm normal.

"

Robin Williams

In 1867, San Francisco instituted America's first "ugly law", which prohibited unsightly people from showing their faces in public.

(It's since been repealed.)

San Francisco still has some strange laws on the books.

For example, you can't walk more than eight dogs at a time, and you can't carry a basket of bread uncovered.

It used to be legal to go anywhere in SF in your birthday suit, but since the passage of the Weiner Law (yes, really) in 2012, nudity is only permitted in specific locations and at permitted events (try Halloween in the Castro).

You can still hang out in the buff at the north end of Baker Beach, if that's your thing.

The annual Folsom Street Fair, held since 1984, is the largest BDSM and Leather subculture gathering in the world, attracting over a quarter of a million people to what is one of the weirdest urban festivals anywhere and definitely not for the fainthearted.

In September 1859,
San Francisco's favorite
eccentric resident, Joshua
Abraham Norton, declared
himself America's emperor.

Emperor Norton had
a following: nearly 30,000
people later packed the
streets for his funeral.

Since 1902, it's been illegal to be buried in San Francisco, due to space limitations.

The only remaining cemeteries are historical—one at the Mission San Francisco de Asís and the other the National Cemetery in the Presidio, left from its days as a military base. But there's also a Pet Cemetery there with over 400 graves.

A flock of parrots lives on Telegraph Hill.

The Aquatic Park
off Crissy Field in the
Marina district features
the Wave Organ,
a unique installation that
plays music powered
by the tide.

There's a stone labyrinth on the beach at Land's End. Take the Land's End trail from the Palace of the Legion of Honor down to the shore to find it.

Opened in the late 1800s, the Sutro Baths used to be a privately owned pool but closed in the 1960s.

Now you can visit the ruins (no swimming) and see the Cliff House below with the Camera Obscura nearby.

Secret SF Spots to Explore the Realm of the Senses:

Garden of Fragrance at the SF Botanical Garden

The Garden of Fragrance was originally designed in 1965 as a garden for visually impaired visitors but is open to all. Gentle touching of the plants releases the aromas of species collected from around the world.

The Truhlsen-Marmor Museum of the Eye at Pier 39

Discover how we see the world around us at the world's only free, public museum dedicated to the science of sight.

The Antique Vibrator Museum at "Good Vibrations" on Polk Street

Hidden in this modern vibrator shop is a collection of vintage sex toys dating back to the 1800s. Thrilling then, and still exciting today.

The Institute of Illegal Images in the Mission District

You need to book a tour at blotterbarn.com to visit collector Mark McCloud's museum devoted to blotter art, the imagery on perforated paper that was dipped into LSD, then torn into tabs for distribution. Mark has collected over 400 framed sheets of blotter, from recent releases back to samples from the Summer of Love.

The Secret of San Francisco Sourdough

Rumors swirl about the city's fog playing a role in the taste of its sourdough, cultivating a type of wild bacteria that only exists in San Francisco.

It's an accepted fact that
California miners making
their way north to Canada
after the Gold Rush brought
their sourdough starters with
them, earning the nickname
"sourdoughs", because
they would actually cuddle
with their sourdough starters
on cold nights to keep the
yeast active.

The Boudin Bakery has been serving sourdough at Fisherman's Wharf since 1849, originally to some of those gold miners, and now primarily to tourists.

San Francisco has a plethora of sourdough bakeries —try Tartine or Acme Breads.

The Buena Vista Café claims to serve more Irish whiskey than any other establishment in the world, thanks to its special recipe for Irish coffee, which may have originated on the Emerald Isle but was perfected in San Francisco.

San Francisco is a food town. Every San Franciscan has their favorite spot with its special dish, whether it's the shrimp salad at Lucca's deli in the Marina or a burrito from La Taqueria in the Mission.

Chef Anthony Bourdain was reportedly partial to the Chinese Mai Tais at Li Po, a dive bar in Chinatown that has been serving drinks since the 1940s.

66

Anyone who doesn't
have a great time in
San Francisco is pretty
much dead to me. You
go there as a snarky
New Yorker thinking it's
politically correct,
it's crunchy granola,

it's vegetarian, and it surprises you every time. It's a two-fisted drinking town, a carnivorous meat-eating town, it's dirty and nasty and wonderful.

"

Anthony Bourdain, chef and TV presenter

Stella Pastry in North Beach is known for its unique Sacripantina Cake, which some claim is perfection made from eggs, cream, air and magic. Sounds like San Francisco.

"

San Francisco has
only one drawback—
'tis hard to leave.

"

Rudyard Kipling, author

If you close your eyes and think of San Francisco, you might hear music, laughter, perhaps a cable car's bell. But the most memorable sound for any summertime visitor is the mournful wail of foghorns from the Golden Gate.

The horns sound for an average of two and half hours year round, but that increases to over 5 hours in the foggy summer months.

When singer Tony Bennett performed his last concert ever in New York City in 2021, he ended the show with the song that has become both his hallmark and an anthem for SF, "I Left my Heart in San Francisco".

66

One day if I go to heaven … I'll look around and say 'It ain't bad. But it ain't San Francisco.'

99

Herb Caen, San Francisco newspaper columnist